IN THE EYE OF THE BEHOLDER

In the Eye of the Beholder

Five True Stories with a Wink, a Nod, and a Tear

T. D. Knopf-Bigelow

Contents

Photography Index

Preface

The following true stories are primarily from my own experiences as a civilian investigator or advocate. One, "Where Did All You Guys Come From?" is from a purely journalistic investigation, desirous of showing the intimate connection between people and critters.

I have always believed in volunteerism, returning to the community at large that which has been given to you in many ways by others. Service to others. I started that belief with involvement in the YMCA. Years later, that would evolve into Crime/Domestic Victim Advocacy and Chief Investigator for a statewide humane society. Professionally, I have served my country as a peace officer as well as a government civil rights investigator. Both man and beast have been focal points in my avocations. Both must be protected.

I hope you enjoy these stories as much as I did living them.

Thomas D. Knopf-Bigelow
Minneapolis

Acknowledgements

The impetus for my involvement is always God.
I speak here of the Triune God of Christianity.
For me all honor and glory must be focused on God the Father,
His Son Jesus, and the Holy Spirit.
Deo Gratias!

Special Thanks:
To my parents, *Glenn and Betty Knopf,*
in memoriam
persons of honesty and integrity.
To *Alice Williams,*
in memoriam
who patiently and faithfully trusted in the Lord to answer
one prayer. She never lost hope.
To *G. I. "Jerry" Hoilien,*
in memoriam
retired Supervisor, Iowa DNR enforcement;
for a lifetime of humor, encouragement, and support. I give

thanks to all your years with mom and dad.
To *Dallas Drake*,
retired firefighter, author, activist,
singer, and friend.
Always encouraging and upbeat.
To *Vinh Tran*
for his constant support, love, and care.
To *Bill Collins*
for his encouragement and foreword.
To *Will Beauchemin*
for his analytical read and timely suggestions.
To *Corinne Dwyer*, editor and president
of North Star Press of St. Cloud, Inc., for all her help and
advice.

This was the author's professional logo when conducting investigations as an independent paralegal-investigator.

The magnifying glass represents investigations. The feather represents two facets of the author's enjoyment and life: first as a quill in writing, second as a symbol of the author's Native American heritage on his mother's side of the family (Ojibwe).

Foreword

Bill Collins

It is tempting to compare Thomas Knopf-Bigelow to G.K. Chesterton's immortal Fr. Brown. Both are men of the cloth with twinkling eyes and warm and gentle natures that belie a courious mind, keen intellect, and a nose for trouble.

While Fr. Brown is as he appears, a simple man who leads the linear and provincial life of a parish priest, rarely straying from the rectory gate, Msgr. Thomas's path is like that of the family dog let loose in the city. He bounds from one adventure to another.

Msgr. Thomas and I became friends swapping stories with a cast of regulars at a local coffee shop. Like my morning tea, the longer Msgr. Thomas steeped the richer and more intense his stories became. The tales told in this book are but a few of the gems kept in the treasure chest of his many and varied adventures.

Not only has Msgr. Thomas been blessed with a kaleidoscope of experiences but also with a storyteller's instinct and humor.

I suggest you poor yourself a cup of hot tea and let Msgr. Thomas steep forth with this delightful and varied collection of true tales.

Bill Collins
Director Operations, Minnesota Actors Theatre
Programming Consultant, NBC Entertainment - Burbank, CA

Chapter One

"Mug" Shot

In early May of 1991, I came face to face with evil. That was the beginning of a six-month-long escapade riddled with anger, frustration, anxiety, hope, and finally, resolution. I was attending a small party at the apartment of an acquaintance from work—beer and ten or fifteen young people.

Shortly after my arrival a group of four or five men came through the front door. One stood out amongst the others, a tall model-looking type beauty, a magnificent physique, wearing a green tank top with burgeoning muscles beneath. He was gorgeous. There's an old adage, "Better to keep your mouth shut and appear stupid than to open it and remove all doubt."[1] Well, Mr. Gorgeous was too young to have learned that one yet.

Someone asked him if it was true that he had been out the prior weekend beating up on gays? Mr.

Gorgeous immediately acknowledged the question with relish. "Yeah, I was looking for fag parties, and they're real easy to find. Just follow them right into the place and beat 'em up. It's great! They don't even fight back or anything."

My insides curdled at his glee and candor. Then he said, "It was so much fun, I'm going back out again this weekend!" The crowd around him lent no support, and a few groaned. It didn't matter to him. He just stood there in his naked pride. I said nothing and just steamed inside. To myself I said, "Your ass is mine!"

The next day, I learned Gorgeous' full name from the acquaintance who invited me. During the next several days I opened a file and began an investigation. The main problem was that there was no body. With no *corpus delicti*, no victim, there is no crime. At this point, all I had was a braggart.

I had worked a couple gay bashings as a victim's advocate. I already had established discrete lines of communications within the gay and lesbian community. Now I was challenged to encounter the gay and lesbian community-at-large. With feelers out on the streets to organizations and individuals, a victim eventually surfaced and called me.

As I waited for the victim's call, many questions came to mind: Would the victim be strong enough to follow through if that was the assailant? Would he recognize the photographs of the suspect? Would fear force him to run from a prolonged court battle?

And then a soft-spoken "James" called me, quietly asking if I was the one who had a suspect description? Initially his description fit to a "T." We agreed to meet at a neutral location, Embers on Hennepin and Twenty-sixth that evening. This time my insides churned for a different reason. I now owned the questions: Would I be willing to go the long hall through the court system, considering my private caseload? Would the enforcement and court systems play ball fairly or would this get thrown out right at the beginning?

What I discovered when I met James was a tall, blond, blue-eyed, intelligent young man of soft-spoken voice and ready smile. He had been one of many attending a weekend after-bar party in the Whittier neighborhood. A fun spring evening for James ended in a nightmare of mental torture, fear for life, and pain, a pain which would endure years after the attack, long after the physical scars healed. Gorgeous and his assistant had chased and cornered James in the entryway of an apartment building. For forty-five minutes, James was taunted with sexual questions, accusations, and told how he was going to die. Before the ordeal was over, Mr. Gorgeous placed a full round-house punch directly to James' left ear and head. The concussion and direct impact of a ring on Gorgeous' hand tore completely through the ear and fractured cartilage. It left James stunned, bleeding, and unable to move. He was momentarily out on his feet, swaying. James never had a chance. He didn't see it coming because of a lack of peripheral vision in his left eye.

It was 5:45 a.m. when Gorgeous and his friend ran away. A passing motorcyclist picked up James and drove him one block to his car. James was afraid his assailants were still lurking in the area. As the bike neared his car, Gorgeous and his accomplice appeared briefly in the single head light beam and disappeared. The weekend party that James attended was the same weekend that Gorgeous had bragged about going out for another go at "fag bashing." Well, now, here was the needed corpus delicti.

More and more peculiar twists and turns came about as the case developed. The couple who hosted the party, Cameron and Shana, were not only eye-witnesses to the attack on James, they were also eye witnesses to another attack on two men by Gorgeous and his accomplice that same night. From those developments, I was able to develop many witnesses and affidavits placing Gorgeous and his buddy at the party.

All three attack victims and the two eye-witnesses were willing to brave the legal system. Fortunately, I was referred to a gay-sensitive police detective to work the case. Victims, witnesses, and myself showed up for a group meeting at the police department and, as Sherlock Holmes would say, "Watson, the game is afoot!" The end of that meeting produced a comment from the detective: "In all my years of police work, I've never had a case just handed to me with a ribbon tied around it. The only thing to do now is go out and arrest the guy."

It was a month and a half before the summons was mailed to Gorgeous. It took that long for the criminal complaints to pass through the City Attorney's office, transfer to the County Attorney's office, and re-transfer to the City Attorney. Numerous prosecutors had bounced it back and forth like a hot potato. This was the first case of an adult prosecution under Minnesota's Hate Crimes Act of 1987, and no one wanted to bite into what they considered a bitter assignment.

Two highlights occurred in the midst of the downtown legal tempest. The day our complaint was signed and issued, a large rally was held called, "Bashers Get Caught," the brainchild of local activist Dallas Drake. It was held in the same neighborhood where the assaults occurred. Only the gay media and KARE 11 TV attended.

The *Star Tribune* and the *Pioneer Press* failed to show on an invite, as did other news outlets. Two unexpected guests did show. Just announced nationwide on CNN, the first woman speaker of the Minnesota House, Representative Dee Long, showed up and addressed the crowd of two hundred. So, also, did a man angrily brandishing a baseball bat.

I suppose I'll leave the aftermath of that story for another time. I would say, though, that the crowds' emotional level was highly enlivened with his appearance. Imagine, celebrating the charging of a serial gay basher, while simultaneously having a weapon of common use against the gay community being brandished at us, a crowd of two hundred.

"Mr. Friendly" left the scene in the company of Minneapolis police wearing shiny but tacky bracelets, all to the accompaniment of a huge, cheering crowd. The cops were glad to get out of there.

And what about Mr. Gorgeous? He failed to show for his first summons, so an arrest warrant was issued. The sheriff couldn't find him because they didn't have his summer address in the Whittier neighborhood. I called and provided that information. Before I left home, immediately after calling the sheriff, I called the detective on our case and told the sergeant how much I would love to be "the mouse in the corner" when Gorgeous was taken and led away.

Needing some cash, I stopped at the Super America store on Lyndale and Twenty-second Street. As I turned away from the instant cash machine, there stood Gorgeous! He was in need of groceries, too. Within seconds, the cashier had been ordered to punch her register keys like a run down robot, one by one. She had a line of fifteen surly anxious customers. A great delay tactic. As police raced to the store (five counts on the arrest warrant), customers fumed. Just as the first squad arrived, out steps Gorgeous with an armload of groceries. The young rookie officer told the somewhat shocked Gorgeous to: ". . . put the bags on the hood and assume the position. You're under arrest."

Three months later, after rancorous legal maneuvers by his defense counsel, Gorgeous pleaded guilty to two counts of gross misdemeanor Bias Crime Assault. He entered into Minnesota's legal history as, *Minnesota v. David Scott Campbell*, the first adult conviction under the state Hate Crimes Act.

To this day, I have a photo of Gorgeous, AKA Campbell, sitting handcuffed in the back of that squad car enameled to my favorite coffee "mug."

"In Germany they came first for the communists, and I didn't speak up because I wasn't a communist. Then they came for the Jews, and I didn't speak up because I wasn't a Jew. Then they came for the trade unionists, and I didn't speak up because I wasn't a trade unionist. Then they came for the Catholics, and I didn't speak up because I was a Protestant. Then they came for me, and by that time no one was left to speak up."[2]

[1]Attributed to Mark Twain (1835-1910)
[2]Attributed to Martin Niemöller (1892-1984), chief pastor, Lutheran Church of Germany.

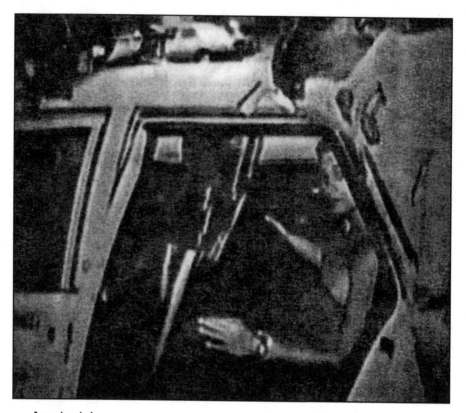

Apprehended.

Chapter Two

In His Own Good Time

The most gratifying investigation I ever accomplished occurred in 1991. I was working for attorneys exclusively as their paralegal-investigator, doing criminal and civil law cases. That investigation clearly showed how God answers prayers in His own good time.

My task—locate the missing family of Betty Knopf, an adopted woman. The grave need was that her youngest son—a husband and father of two—was in dire need of a kidney transplant. His mother, Betty, who had been adopted as a child, had no knowledge of her family or its medical history. Having that medical history was a necessity because it would allow doctors to make the best decisions on treatment and better understand potential hazards.

Up to that time Betty had opposed all attempts to research her family history. She had made it poignantly clear that she had no intention of dishonoring the memory of her adoptive father and mother. They were the only parents she had ever known. She had been devoted to them throughout her life as well as in their passing. Now her own flesh and blood, her youngest one, was critically ill. A higher priority had appeared, and that's where I came in. Let me put the cart-before-the-horse and tell what I found out. Then I'll describe how I came to that discovery.

*   *   *   *

Betty-Jean was born in 1928 to an impoverished Native American family that had become a single-parent family with six children. One of the children, a son, had tragically died in a sledding accident. Food was scarce. That's when the county social services stepped in and forced the issue: either take them all to the "Indian" school in Michigan or give them to the orphanage.

Betty's natural mother chose Michigan, loading her five children into a Model-T Ford and traveling the long, arduous trip, cross-country from North Central Minnesota, on two-track dirt roads to Detroit. When they finally got there, the school made an error in calculating the correct percentage of "Indian" blood and rejected them. There was only one remaining option—return to Minnesota. On the round trip, Betty-Jean was held on the lap of the oldest child, Alice, fourteen years old or the second oldest, Daisy, twelve years old. David was eight, and Myrtle was four.

Alice and Betty. (Bigelow family archive)

Back in Minnesota the children were turned over to the state and placed into the Owatonna Orphanage and High School. Imagine the pain and sadness their mother suffered! Betty-Jean was immediately separated from the other children and put into the nursery. Polio was not preventable, treatable or curable at this point in the century, and fear was rampant that an epidemic might go like fire through the orphanage. So, the youngest and most adoptable, the infants, were permanently separated from contact with all other children, even siblings. Alice and Daisy could only look through a window at Betty-Jean. That was how Daisy saw Betty-Jean take her first steps.

Then, just days before Christmas, Betty-Jean disappeared, vanished. The orphanage staff didn't feel any need or obligation to tell Alice and Daisy what had happened to their baby sister. Was she dead? Was she adopted? Was she hurt? Alice, being the oldest, felt a deep guilt. She felt personally responsible for the kids. "We were supposed to be together as a family," she insisted. She would carry this guilt throughout her adult life. Eventually they learned that a good family had adopted Betty-Jean. Sadly, this was the first of many Christmases without their little sister. Their hearts ached: Were Betty-Jean's new parents kind to her? Did they love her? Did she lack for anything? Did she know or remember anything of the other kids? There were so many unanswered questions, regrets and feelings of loss. After Betty's disappearance, the children made a pact between

Charles and Baby Betty. (Bigelow family archive)

themselves—never to go home with anyone or be adopted.

* * * *

Charles and Alice Bigelow, married several years, lived in Austin, Minnesota. Alice was unable to bear children, and, so, adoption was their only hope. He was a senior executive with the Geo. A. Hormel Co. They lived well and had much to offer a child; they were well respected in business, their community, and their church. So, they placed their name on the orphanage list.

Early one winter morning, just days before Christmas, the orphanage called. They had five children. Would they like to come up and see them? Mrs. Bigelow got into the car and drove the difficult thirty miles North in a harsh Minnesota blizzard.

13

One thing, though, she had failed to call the office and tell her husband that she was taking this excursion. Once at the orphanage, she had no trouble deciding quickly that Betty-Jean was the one.

With Betty-Jean wrapped and bundled into the Buick, Mrs. Bigelow set out again into the winter storm. All the way back Mrs. Bigelow talked to baby Betty. Something or Someone had moved Mrs. Bigelow. Imagine the look on Charles' face as he came through the back door after work, only to realize he was an instant father. Unfortunately, the Bigelows had not anticipated such a short notice from the orphanage. They had no supplies, clothes, bedding, or toys.

The next day, a Saturday, Mrs. Bigelow spent the whole morning shopping for all the child's necessities. All morning little Betty sat on a tiny wooden footstool looking at Charles Bigelow wondering, *Who is this new man?* Every once in a while Betty would say to him, "Momma come. Momma come," referring to Alice. She had bonded beautifully with her new mom on that long trip home. And it wasn't long before she knew that she was the apple of her new dad's eye.

*   *   *   *

Back at the orphanage, David died at fourteen, five years after Betty was adopted. The second oldest, Daisy, had been loaned out to a farm family as a child laborer, a frequent and often sad occurrence at the

Betty and Rumpus. (Bigelow family archive)

orphanage. Abuses often followed. On learning that David was dying, the farmer refused to let Daisy return; nor would he allow her to go to the funeral. She was under a contract with the orphanage—that was that.

All three remaining sisters eventually left the orphanage, lived for a short time with grandparents in the Northwest, and eventually were reunited with family in Michigan. Their birth mother was also reunited with those girls and was able to share many of her remaining years with them until her death at nearly one hundred years of age. Throughout those years, the unanswered questions about Betty-Jean lingered. The sisters were all married, some with children of their own. There

15

were many hard times. For Alice, though, her faith in the Lord remained solid. Her prayers and hopes were that the Lord would allow her some knowledge of what happened to baby Betty-Jean before Alice went to her final rest. Three sisters and now a half brother were spread out all over the country: Michigan, Missouri, New Mexico, and California.

*   *   *   *

Betty at graduation, 1945.
(Bigelow family archive)

The growing years for Betty were filled with love. All her needs and more were met. During her senior year in high school, her beloved father suddenly passed unto the Lord. At the time, Charles and Alice had been on a business trip in Syracuse, New York, and Betty was working at a summer camp in Yellow Stone. It was a long and sad return to Minnesota for both daughter and mother.

Not long after Betty's father died, Betty married Glenn, a wounded World War II veteran. They had a simple wedding ceremony in Betty's home with a distant relative, a foreign missionary pastor of two decades, tying the knot. The years passed with Betty and Glenn having three sons, and in time, four grandchildren.

16

Betty and Charles at graduation. (Bigelow family archive)

Charles Bigelow, circa 1945. (Bigelow family archive)

Betty and Glenn's wedding photo. Left to right: Marg Knowlton, Betty and Glenn, and G. I. "Jerry" Hoilien. (Bigelow family archive)

*   *   *   *

That's the cart-before-the-horse version. The investigation into locating the family was not particularly hard. I had some thirty-year-old leads, no particular talent on my part. Most certainly the hand of the Lord was working His deeds.

I located Alice, seventy-nine years of age, in suburban Detroit, Michigan. It was just a few days after

Alice Bigelow, circa 1960s. (Bigelow family archive)

Betty's family. Front row: Thomas (author); back row: Glenn and Betty, Bill, and Chuck. (Knopf family archives)

Christmas about 8:30 p.m. To this day I regret not having recorded that first conversation. A lot went through my head at the time: Would she, the oldest sister, still be alive these many years later? If so, did she care what had happened to her long-lost sibling? Would she cooperate? Would she slam the phone down in anger or fear?

I dialed the number. It rang. A teeny tiny wee voice answered:

"Hello?" She sounded elderly.

I asked, "Is this Alice Williams?"

"Yes . . . ?"

"Are you sitting down, Mrs. Williams?" I asked cautiously and gently.

"Well, no. Should I be?"

"I think it might be a good idea if you sat down first."

There was a pause as she moved to a chair. Scraping sounds.

"Okay. I'm sitting now."

"Mrs. Williams, does the name Betty-Jean Freeman mean anything to you?"

I heard her gasp and then firmly say, "Yes!"

"Well, Mrs. Williams, this is Betty-Jean Freeman's second oldest son, Thomas, calling."

"OH . . . MY . . . GOD . . . I'VE BEEN WAITING FOR THIS PHONE CALL FOR SIXTY-THREE YEARS!"

I can assure you there was a flood of tears on both sides of the phone line and many questions asked. Well over half a century of distance was closed with that single phone call. Alice's prayers for Betty to be safe and returned to her had been answered.

Happily, mom has been able to meet two of her three sisters. Mom is now glad that a veil on her history was pulled aside and all are the better for it.

Yes, He does work in mysterious and wonderful ways. When we put the prayer before Him, He determines when and how to answer that prayer. Our task is to keep that faith. Alice sure did. Amen!

Betty and older sister Alice Williams reunited, circa 1994. (Knopf family archive)

Epilogue

This story is dedicated to the memory of Alice Williams who returned to the Lord in the fall of 1998. Quietly and suddenly she was taken from her favorite garden to a reward well deserved.

Betty's funeral, Msgr. Thomas, celebrant and author. (Courtesy of Liliane Vangay)

Chapter Three

What Child Is This We Crucified?

Preface

The following poem came after the resolution of a "Wrongful Death" law case a number of years ago. I had been assigned by an attorney to investigate the death of a severely mentally and physically handicapped adult residing in a group home. Initially a finding of death by natural causes was given by the medical examiner. After a request for review, based on my investigative results, the death was changed to death by unnatural causes. Federal and state authorities investigated a psychiatrist, a nurse, and the director of the facility.

This was one of the most difficult cases I have ever investigated. Five years after my involvement, I awoke on a Good Friday morning reciting the beginning of the poem. I continued writing for three days. I chose to juxtapose prose with Biblical verse, paralleling the patient's death process with that of Our Lord, Jesus Christ. The patient was a child of God, and what happened in this death should not have happened to anyone. I hope that this chronicle, albeit painful and dark in reading, will remind us of our responsibility to the least of His flock. Scriptural references are from the New Jerusalem Bible.

The Author

Nan was not us.
From birth she was,
at best,
our worst.
A brain impaired to function,
she relied upon all
for her every need.

Nan stayed at home,
under parental care
her first years of life,
until time consumed all
in the family.

Language as we know and
communicate with,
did not exist for Nan.
She could love,
reach out,
but most of her existence
was within her limited sphere
of reason and concept.

Hearts were gripped and
squeezed with pain,
knowing they couldn't handle
Nan's care.
A move was needed.

"I tell you solemnly,
in so far as you did this to one of the least
of these brothers of mine,
you did it to me."[1]

Home became a house founded
by similar parents,
to care for their like children.

Staff around the clock,
to feed,
cloth,
comfort.

A nurse to see to
their medical needs,
albeit at times,
from afar.

For Nan,
special meds were needed,
psychotropics,
to keep her even.

Harsh upon anyone,
it was necessary
by the home's psychiatrist;
one on the outer edge
of his profession.

Nan needed more special attention
and care on this med.

The staff needed special training
to use this med,
something they never received.
To that end,
Nan would be lost.

*"I tell you solemnly,
in so far as you did this to one of the least . . ."*[2]

Over a year and a half,
Nan received this drug.
None were the wiser
to its dangers and signs.

When someone at the home
would act out,
the staff called it
"behaviors."

Patients
acted inappropriately.
Discipline must be present.

For Nan,
"behaviors" existed
because of her special med.

Over time, and inappropriate
dose fluctuations,
she reacted.

"Harshly dealt with,
he bore it humbly,
he never opened his mouth . . ."[3]

In time,
Nan became more dependent,
lost weight,
refused to eat.

One who loved and cared,
would sit and patiently
try to feed her.

She was admonished;
told to disregard.
Nan had "behaviors."
Something was wrong!

". . . like a lamb that is led
to the slaughter-house,
like a sheep that is dumb
before its shearers,
never opening its mouth."[4]

Over months,
Nan lost forty pounds.
Her meds were jumped
and decreased.

Her brain,
unable to adjust.

The long "hour" of crucifixion had come.

"... *And sadness came over him.*
and great distress."[5]

She would not go
peacefully into the night.
She was restless,
irritable.
"Behaviors."

It was for those who care,
to be mindful of her needs.

Her body cried out for relief,
and yet they understood not.

"Be on your guard,
stay awake,
because you never know
when the time will come."[6]

Crouched in the bathroom,
a foot in the toilet,
Nan could not fend for herself.

Panting,
Kicking,
Put to bed.

It was after midnight.
The house was down
and quiet.

"You should be awake,
and praying not to be put to the test.
The spirit is willing,
but the flesh is weak."[7]

They saw,
but did not understand.
Why was Nan acting
like this?

Nan was confused.
She used hand signs:
"Coffee,"
"Shaver,"
"Dress,"
"Brush teeth."

She threw off her attends.

"And when they had finished
making fun of him,
they took off the cloak."[8]

They knew not what they saw.

"I call all the day,
My God,
But you never answer."[9]

A call was placed to the nurse.
More meds were approved.

"I tell you solemnly,
one of you is about to
betray me."[10]

She found no solace.

"Pull me out of the net
they have spread for me."[11]

She carried on,
unabated,
flailing her limbs,
from side to side.

On and on.
For hours.

Again,
the nurse was called.

Waiting.

More meds.

Nan in the grinder;
bruises on her cheeks,
redness,
rug burns:
on shoulders,
neck,
ankles,
hips.

"... *for huge as the sea,
is your affliction;
who can possibly
cure you?*"[12]

The nurse called back.
She'd stop by;
after work,
in the morning.

The staff were frightened.
Nothing worked for Nan.
Worry . . .

Another call is placed.
Awoken was the director.
"Not to worry,"
says she.

"*. . . and Peter remembered*
what Jesus had said,
'Before the cock crows
you will have disowned me
three times.'"[13]

Her face was ashen,
eyes wild,
vomiting blood.

"*My God,*
My God,
Why have you deserted me?"[14]

A blanket was given
to her.

"*. . . and made him wear*
a scarlet cloak . . ."[15]

The one who cared
and loved her,
came on duty.

Just through
the front door,
she knew what she saw.
She could see Death's approach.
She'd seen it before.

Then,
Nan's body slowed,
decreased its fight;
still very ashen.

A second call was made
to the director.

A plea for help.
"Let me call the ambulance;
she's dying!"

"No,
You're over reacting,
distraught.
I'll call the parents.
You know not what you see."

Conscious,
coherent,
very ashen.
Quiet.

Blood pressure
50/20.
The first ever taken
all night.

And then,
just as the
one who cared
returned from the phone—
admonished,
rebuked,

. . . Nan breathed her last . . .

CPR was started.
911 called,
EMS arrived;
Police,

Fire,
Paramedics.
More drugs.
Scissors cut a shirt
for access to the heart.

"At that,
the veil of the temple
was torn in two
from top to bottom . . ."[16]

The parents walked in.
Nan at thirty-three,
was gone.

"And many women
were there,
watching from a distance,
the same women
who had followed Jesus
from Galilee
and looked after him."[17]

How could this be?
How did this happen?
We were here.

"So Joseph took the body,
wrapped it in a clean shroud
and put it in his own new tomb . . ."[18]

Only in His time
will we meet Nan
without her Earthen wear;
no longer a broken vessel,

spent chard's of pottery;
from the floor rug
to the autopsy table.

" I saw the Holy City,
and the New Jerusalem,
coming down from God
out of heaven,
as beautiful as a bride
all dressed for her husband."[19]

Nan awaits us.
To forgive us.

Notes

[1]Matt 25:40
[2]Ibid.
[3]Isa 53:7a
[4]Isa 53:7b
[5]Matt 26:37
[6]Mk 13:33
[7]Matt 26:41
[8]Matt 27:31
[9]Pslm 22:2
[10]Matt 26:21
[11]Pslm 31:4a

[12]Lam 2:13
[13]Matt 26.75
[14]Matt 27:46
[15]Matt 27:28
[16]Matt 27:51
[17]Matt 27:55
[18]Matt 27:59
[19]Rev 21:2

Chapter Four

"Where Did All You Guys Come From?"

Burnsville, Minnesota, is a city divided, divided by Highway I-35W into an East-West community of 55,000 souls. It is a spry, quickly growing bedroom community south of Minneapolis, one whose edges touch both metropolitan and rural areas. Expansion is the word commonly used in referring to this city, and Burnsville is proud of its law enforcement and fire protection services.

Monday, August 3rd, 1992. Captain Jay Knutson of the Burnsville Fire Department was on duty at Fire Station No. 2, two blocks behind the Minnesota Valley Humane Society shelter. At twelve noon, the station alarm and radio paging tones activated. Station 2 received a medical response call for the Medic 2 Fire Ambulance—an emergency transfer to the hospital.

Minnesota Valley Humane Society shelter. (Author photo)

On the west side of town, veteran fire motor operator (FMO) Dallas Drake proudly checked over the latest addition to Station No. 1's fire department motor pool: a new Peterbilt fire engine/pumper. This beast coming down the road looked like a massive, illuminated semitruck with the whole of the fire department attached.

Down the street from Station 2, the newly built Minnesota Valley Humane Society shelter opened to the public at noon, just as Medic 2 wailed and sped by. The shelter had come into existence because the City of Burnsville and Dakota County recognized and affirmed the impact and interplay of "man (sic) and beast."

Burnsville Fire Station 2 sign. (Author photo)

Executive Director Dean Weigl joined in the day's opera-tion amidst a cacophony of noise, as did the many volun-teers throughout the day and year.

Camille McArdle, D.V.M., began her day as the chief veterinary officer for the Canterbury Downs horse track, responsible for the medical and humane treatment of horses. Her spouse, Roy Dawson, worked as a veteran cop with Burnsville, as well as a reserve fire fighter. Later that evening, Roy was home on a rare night off. He and Camille enjoyed each other's company, playing couch potato in front of the TV.

For a man called Chester, it was a night out with his dog, quality time for each other. For the pooch, it was a long day's anticipation and patient waiting ending in a happy walk.

Located directly across Highway 13 from the humane society is the American Boarding Kennels. AB Kennels had already discharged most of its four-legged weekend boarders. That night, Linda Phillips was in charge of the now quieter operation.

*   *   *   *

At 8:40 p.m. Station No. 1 received an alarm. Medic 1 and their new pumper were dispatched to a car accident with injuries. Many thoughts automatically went through the fire fighters' minds, most of them unspoken: Is there fire? Are we going to have to pry the victim out? Are the people involved alive? Is traffic control set up?

Station 2 apparatus. (Author photo)

45

Chester leashed his dog for the nightly constitutional. A clear warm August evening brought a variety of noises and scents to the ears and nose of Chester's pal. I don't know where the phrase, "Man's (sic) best friend" originates, but Chester and pal symbolized that partnership and harmony. It was 8:30 p.m. as they walk down the darkened streets. They passed among the true golden factors of Burnsville, its people. As they passed by the humane society shelter, Chester smelled the hint of burning wood and saw smoke coming off the roof. *Something's just not right*, thought Chester. "Come on, let's go." he said to his pal.

Fire Captain Knutson was on the phone when Chester and pal came in through the main vehicle bay. Chester explained his observations of smoke and the odor of burning wood. He was concerned. Knutson immediately hung up the phone and punched into the direct phone line of the Fire/Police Dispatch.

After the phone was back in its cradle, Knutson hollered for everyone in Station 2 to mount up. Station house lights in Stations 1 and 2 flickered on automatically. A series of alert tones echoed throughout each station house, and the fire dispatcher's voice sounded out:

"45-273, REPORT OF SMOKE COMING FROM A BUILDING AT 131 HWY. 13, THE MINNESOTA VALLEY HUMANE SOCIETY. REPORT FROM A PASSER-BY OF SMOKE. 2037 HOURS."

Dean Weigl had just finished a meeting at the shelter; the last staffer had left ten minutes earlier. The shelter had been closed to the public for little more than thirty minutes. In the hallway, Dean caught the smell of smoke. A haze clouded the air. The unthinkable was reality: FIRE! Dean moved quickly to call 911. By this time Chester and pal had already raised the alarm.

Dean was only off the phone to 911 momentarily when the first fire units arrived. He quickly gathered up leashes and collars. Captain Knutson was the first through the door as other "fire eaters" outside suited up and charged a hose line.

Knutson was unfamiliar with the new facility, and the interior doors were unmarked. Methodically he moved and checked each door for heat and smoke. He soon realized that the animals had to be gotten out quickly, and many a hand would be needed. He called for a third alarm—a call-out of the volunteer reserves for that shift. Would it be enough? Fast enough? Pagers city-wide went off with the fire dispatcher's voice:

"THREE-ALARM, COMPANY B CALL OUT.
REPORT TO YOUR RESPECTIVE
STATIONS."

A mile and a half away, Roy Dawson's pager activated. Camille immediately recognized the shelter's address and decided she had better go along. There might be a need for emergency care—or euthanasia. The Emergency Clinic down the road from the shelter could provide supplies.

After throwing empty cages into their pickup, Roy and Camille headed for the fire scene. "We expected the worst possible situation as we approached," Camille recalled.

Captain Knutson located the fire and sent a team in to extinguish it. Then he grabbed two dogs and headed for the back door. Outside he could see people milling about from the neighborhood. He motioned a couple people over to take charge of the two dogs. They responded quickly, and he returned for more. The roof was being checked for hot spots. The actual fire was extinguished quickly. More water was used to charge the hose than used on the fire. But, in the process of extinguishing the flames, more smoke was created, causing an increased concern for the tolerance levels of the remaining animals.

As Roy and Camille approach, there were lines of people walking dogs along the road away from the fire scene. They couldn't believe their eyes! Camille took up triage at the back door and told Captain Knutson that the cats had to get out faster to survive. Knutson quickly made another call to dispatch, a call that would bring out every fire fighter in the city. Many levels of tonal alerts pierced the night air:

"4th ALARM CALL OUT. REPORT
TO YOUR RESPECTIVE STATIONS."

Captain Knutson returned a second time to the back door with two more dogs. There were lines of people waiting to take them. Handing them over, Knutson had no idea where they were going. He could see many of the neighborhood people walking dogs toward the Dairy Queen next door. Later he recounted, "I thought they were taking them over there to get a DQ to calm them down."

The real miracle occurring was that legions of neighborhood people appeared. As fast as the fire fight-

Dallas Drake (Courtesy of Dallas Drake)

ers extricated animals, people were taking them in hand calmly, orderly, quickly moving them out of danger with-out hesitation.

Fortunately, Dean Weigl had the foresight to pre-arrange an emergency action plan. The AB Kennels would provide shelter. A fast phone call, and all was arranged by Linda Phillips. Linda and staffers quickly isolated their present boarders to another area, widening spaces for the inbound refugees. By the time she got to the front door, the whole parking lot was filled with "man and beast" (sic). In Linda's typical orderly fashion, she had all the critters lined up single file (two-legged and four-legged) taking the dogs inside two by two. She later remarked, "It was like Noah's Ark, by the two's." Linda asked a few people at the front door, "Where did all you guys come from?"

One person responded, "We were just driving down the highway and saw the fire trucks at the humane society, so we thought we'd stop and see if they needed some help . . ." Another said: "We live across the street from the shelter and saw the trucks and thought, 'Maybe they could use a hand', so, we walked over . . ."

*   *   *   *   *

In order to work the interior of the shelter, fire fighters had to use full "turn out" gear, including the self-contained "Scott" air packs. The first cat brought out, an adult, was terrified. FMO Drake had the job of delivering this feline. Drake tried to talk to the cat to calm it down, but, according to Drake, he probably looked and sounded to puss like Darth Vadar from Spielberg's *Star Wars* movie. In his first attempt Drake tried holding the cat by the midsection—not. The cat was loose in a second. Again Drake took the feline by the midsection. The cat meant business! It sank its teeth into Drake's wrist. This was no small feat. Puss's teeth had to go through his fire jacket, wrist protector, glove—and then home to warm flesh. In fact, Drake said puss stayed attached that way until they got outside.

Over and over, people made trips between the shelter and AB Kennels. According to Captain Knutson, "Most people panic at a fire scene when there is nothing to do, when there is no hope. At this scene, people worked as a living, breathing conveyor belt." Many if not most were young people in their teens.

The last critter removed was the shelter's "house cat." This feline refused to abandon ship. Only after the fire was out, with everyone thinking that he was lost . . . who turned up? Talk about nine lives! He had some minor smoke inhalation problems, but, after a night at the Emergency Clinic, he fared just fine.

Epilogue

In all, eighty animals were rescued. The terrified cat removed by FMO Drake calmed down once inside the

Saint Francis of Assisi, patron saint of animals. (Author photo)

AB Kennels. There were no repercussions from having bitten Drake, although secret sources stated that a four-teen-day rabies watch was kept on Drake just in case the cat needed treatment. All the animals were returned to the humane society the next afternoon—after a lot of cleaning up and airing out. A follow-up investigation revealed that a burner on an unused stove in a storeroom had been accidentally turned on. The actual fire damage was confined to that storeroom and the appliance.

And what about all those anonymous handlers? How did they fare after stepping forward, giving from the heart in a real time of crisis? Seventy-five to 100 people turned out to save eighty animals. Not an animal was lost, and only one fire fighter suffered any wounds. It says a lot about the people of Burnsville. I don't presume to have the right words to place all those sacrifices into perspective. The known and unknown rescuers of the shelter fire of 1992 demonstrated their hearts and courage in Burnsville, Minnesota.

"45-273 TO DISPATCH. THE FIRE
IS KNOCKED DOWN AND RESCUE IS
COMPLETE. YOU CAN CANCEL
THE 4-ALARM CALL NOW."

Chapter Five

Behind the Bell at Hanscom Chapel

I have always loved bells, especially church bells. As a youngster, a set of Norwegian hand bells had been given to the First Congregational Church in memory of my paternal great-grandparents. The church also had a large bell in the steeple with the steeple cross in memory of a great-great-grandfather who was pastor of that church in the early 1900s. Bells I know!

For centuries bells have been the "town crier" of news: signaling the start and conclusion of wars, marriages and births, national celebrations and mourning, daily and weekly religious observances. Many civilian personnel don't realize that military bases have active vibrant chapels representing most religions—living communities of ecumenism. Hanscom Air Force Base Chapel joins those centuries of history with its special bell.

In the summer of 1975, I was assigned TDY (temporary duty) by the police squadron to the military

Hanscom AFB Chapel. (Courtesy of Msgr. Thomas Sande, CH., LTC. USAF Ret.)

resort named Fourth Cliff at Scituate, Massachusetts. The resort is actually on a thin strip of land a mile long adjacent to the Scituate Harbor. Technically, it's an island connected to the mainland by two small bridges. Most of the island was set with private summer cottages; the resort sitting at the far tip of the island. In the summer of 1975, the resort had cabins on the leeward side. Camping sites and a large abandoned World War II naval gun emplacement were seaward, evidenced by a large grass berm with metal doors. Centered within the resort proper was a small lodge and staff cabin. It was a run down affair, rustic in comparison to what exists today.

My religious experience at that time was that of a "High Church" Episcopalian, one closely resembling the Roman Catholic tradition. One of those shared traditions was the reciting and ringing of the Angelus bell. In the early church, prior to the Reformation, local churches rang their bells in a special sequence. This occurred at 0600 hours, 1200 hours, and 1800 hours. The same prayer was recited at each of the three hours. It was a means of sanctifying the workday for the peasants. The ancient tradition continues to this day with those churches having bells—real or electronic.

At Fourth Cliff, I wanted to locate a small nautical bell that I could nail to the side of a cabin for recitation of the Angelus. It would also be available if someone wanted to have religious services. We were at the ocean so a small nautical bell seemed appropriate. Something six to seven inches in diameter, similar to what I mounted on wood in my study many years later.

Our bell at Hanscom Base Chapel came through the hands of a retired U.S. Navy Captain (0-6) I met that summer. He was the only permanent resident on that small island. His house was specially constructed for year-round use, and he had a large picture window seaward made of bulletproof glass. A ship's wooden steering wheel stood on the second floor Great Room. One could look out a ship's portal window while going through an internal stairwell.

Thomas and his parents at the bell. (Knopf family archives)

This retiree was heavily decorated, in addition to being the stereotypical supply officer with a colorful history in multiple wars. In his worldwide tours, he made lifetime connections with purveyors of all types of supplies. On final discharge from the navy, he established a business as a broker in world supply commodities.

When I told the captain what I was looking for, he volunteered to put out some "feelers" for a bell. One month later, I got a call to come down to his house; he had something to show me. When I got there, I found this rather large bell, substantially larger and heavier than I could imagine. I sure couldn't "nail" that up on a cabin wall. The bell came off a decommissioned Spanish frigate of the 1800s and was left in the Virgin Islands. It was supposed to be installed in a church on the island. But the church building, in time, was abandoned and a fire destroyed the storage shed with only the bell surviving. That's when it went onto the international buyers market.

What does an aficionado of bells do when landing a big one? Certainly not turn it down! Then it dawned on me—the base chapel didn't have a real bell. When I ran that thought by the captain, he offered to sell the bell to me at cost for shipping. There was a catch, though. I had three days, until Thursday noon, to come up with the money and move the bell out.

On Airman First Class pay, $300 was a lot. I also had to contact the base chaplain, Lieutenant Colonel Nelson, to see if he was allowed to accept such a donation. All said and done, the chaplain said, "Yes"—

Sgt. T.D. Knopf, USAF, directing traffic on Presidential detail.

although he had never received such a donation. A security police pick-up truck was commandeered the morning of the third day for transport. It was the most magnificent ride I ever took in a military vehicle! The captain said that maybe with this bell, St. Peter would think kindly of him when he died and arrived at the "pearly gates," having been a lapsed Christian all these years.

Three hours after the bell left Scituate Island and arrived at Hanscom A.F.B., the captain got a call from a prospective buyer—an offer to buy the bell for $25,000.

I prayerfully hope the "pearlies" were opened wide for the captain's final deployment—with one bell peeling a welcome from within.

He
loved
the
Truth,
and
sought
to
know
it.

On the desk and tombstone of William J. Mayo, M.D.
(1861-1939)

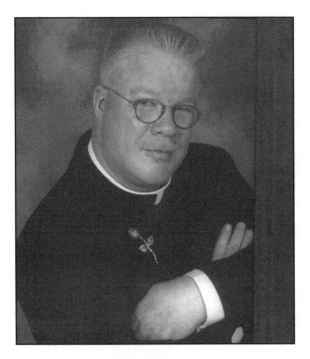

About the Author

Msgr. Knopf-Bigelow, Minneapolis, Minnesota, is a Catholic priest of the Heartland Old Catholic Church. Unlike the fictional character of Fr. Brown in G.K. Chesterton's mystery series, Msgr. Knopf-Bigelow was an investigator long before he became a priest.[1] He is a former peace officer and has extensive civilian experience in the field of investigations, including: criminal and civil law as a paralegal-investigator, civil rights, animal welfare law and enforcement, and insurance. He has also been a crime victim advocate, a school advocate, and a teacher. He is currently pastor of a small parish and volunteers as a law enforcement chaplain. He can be reached at his email address: msgr-thos@scc.net

---

[1] *The Penguin Complete Fr. Brown*, G.K. Chesterton, Penguin Books, 1981.